WORLDfocus

Kenya

DAVID MARSHALL
GEOFF SAYER

Contents

Note to the Reader
Some words in this book are printed in **bold**
type. This shows that the word is listed in the
glossary on page 30. The glossary gives a brief
explanation of words that might be new to you.

Introduction

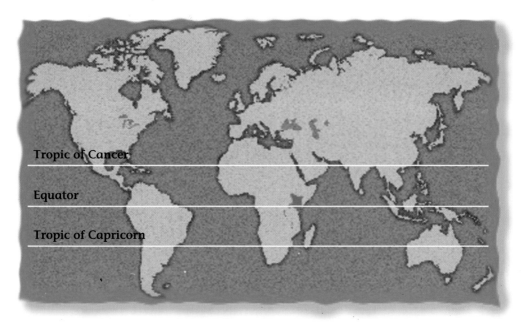

Tropic of Cancer

Equator

Tropic of Capricorn

You may have watched television programs about the wildlife in Kenya, or talked to people who have taken vacations there. If you have, then you may think of Kenya as a country of palm-fringed beaches, snow-topped mountains, and exciting wild animals like lions and leopards, elephants and rhinos, giraffes and wildebeest.

You may have heard of Kenya's capital, Nairobi. It is a busy modern city with shops and hotels, factories and skyscrapers, a university and parliament buildings. If you were only to visit Nairobi, or the beaches and wildlife parks, you would not really know Kenya at all.

Kenya is almost as large as the state of Texas. It lies in East Africa, with a coastline on the Indian Ocean. A striking feature of the landscape is the Rift Valley, which runs for about 2,480 miles through Africa. In Kenya there are highlands on both sides of the Rift Valley, rising to the icy summit of Mount Kenya. At 17,058 feet it is Africa's second highest mountain.

△ **Where is Kenya?**

▽ **Looking across the Rift Valley near Nairobi.**

The Rift Valley has been called the "Cradle of Mankind." Here scientists have found the skeletons and stone tools of early humans. Some of the finds are over 2 million years old. The first human beings may have developed in this part of Africa.

Kenya lies on the equator, so the sun rises at about 7:00 A.M. and sets at about 7:00 P.M. every day of the year. Kenyans do not talk of winter and summer; they talk instead about wet and dry seasons. In most of the country the drier months are between June and September.

Map of Kenya showing the main geographical features.

Close to the coast it is hot and humid, with rain during most of the year. There is good rainfall in the southwest, in the highlands, and around Lake Victoria, too. This area provides much of Kenya's agricultural land.

The highlands are over 4,900 feet above sea-level. At this level the climate is **temperate**. It is warm, but not hot.

The lands to the north and east, which make up over two-thirds of the country, are hotter and drier. Much of this is "bush" country, where people live mainly by keeping cows, goats, sheep, and camels.

3

The People

Today's Kenya is a rich mixture of lifestyles and languages. For over a thousand years, East Africa has been a meeting point for different peoples and different ways of life. Groups of farmers and **herders** moved onto the land from the south and the north. Each group brought its own **culture** with its own dress and building style, music and art, and language and beliefs.

Some groups settled on the coast, looking out onto a wider world. Traders crossing the Indian Ocean brought goods from Arabia, Persia, India, and Indonesia. In this way, bananas first came to East Africa, where they are now widely grown. Small sailing boats called **dhows** came to Mombasa, Malindi, and other ports to buy and sell gold, ivory, cloth, glass, and tools.

Arab influence was strong, and the people on the coast developed a distinct way of life. They became known as the Swahili, an Arabic word meaning "coast-dwellers." Their language, Swahili, was mainly African with a mixture of Arabic. Today it is the national language of Kenya and its neighbor, Tanzania.

△ **Many people settled along Kenya's coast. This is the waterfront at Lamu.**

The Islamic religion also spread along the coast, where it remains strong. **Missionaries** from European churches traveled inland, bringing Christianity. In modern Kenya, over half the people are Christians.

In the last hundred years, life has changed very quickly for the people of East Africa. Before 1895 there was no country called Kenya. People organized themselves within their own groups, or clans. On the coast, there were town governments.

This changed between 1870 and 1914, when European countries invaded Africa. Britain sent its soldiers and took over much of East Africa. They created the colony of Kenya, which was ruled from London. The best land was taken from the Africans by settlers from Britain and became known as the White Highlands. A chief described how this news came to his people: "A Pink Cheek came and told us of his King who lived over the seas. 'This great king is now your king,' he said, 'and this land is all his land.' This was strange news, for the land was ours. . . ."

△ The Jamia mosque in Nairobi where Muslims go to pray.

Kenya finally became an **independent** country in 1963. Jomo Kenyatta led the struggle against British rule and became the first President of the Republic of Kenya.

British rule has left its mark on Kenya. English is widely spoken, and systems of law and government are based on the English way.

Where Do People Live?

Kenya has a population of about 28 million. That means an average of 124 people for each square mile, compared with about 73 in the United States. Almost all Kenya's population is African. There are about 200,000 Kenyans of European, Asian, or Arabic origin.

Kenya's capital, Nairobi, has a population of almost 1.5 million. Other major cities include Kisumu, Nakuru, and the port of Mombasa. A quarter of the population lives in the rapidly growing towns.

If you were to travel around Kenya, you would see many different ways of life. You might see Gabbra people lead their camel trains across the dry northern plains, as they have for centuries. A group of Kamba women sing as they work together, turning over the soil in a corn field with their hoes. A Kikuyu trader piles up cooking pots and brightly-colored plastic bowls on her market stand. Luo children pound cassava roots into flour on a rock beside Lake Victoria. An Asian shopkeeper rearranges the video cassette recorders (VCRs) in his city store to catch the eye of passing customers. A Somali herder milks her goats, calling them out of their pen by name: "Ouley, Bariar, Hale, Jogbela. . ."

▲ Wangoi in Uhuru Park, Nairobi.

Many people have moved from the country to the towns to try to make a better living. Sometimes men come alone looking for work, hoping to send money back to their families. People find jobs in shops, offices, and factories. Others may work as nannies, housekeeping staff, and night watchmen in the wealthy suburbs, or sell newspapers, soft drinks, candy, and peanuts in the city.

Wangoi is ten years old. She came to Nairobi with her mother and brother. They left their small farm when her father died. They live in Kibera, an area of poor housing.

Wangoi describes their life in Nairobi: "Most days I walk into town with my mother, to see what's happening—she's selling peanuts in the park. My brother Mwangi is here too. We don't like Nairobi. We want to go back to Murang'a, to go to school. Mother will take us back when she has enough money—she says, when she's saved enough."

Life can be difficult in the city.

Agriculture

Most people in Kenya are farmers. In the fertile highlands, farms are usually small plots of less than 2.5 acres, about the size of a soccer field.

Many families grow enough corn, bananas, beans, potatoes, and other vegetables to provide food for the whole year. They may have one or two cows for milk and a few chickens. This is known as **subsistence** farming: they produce enough to feed themselves.

People need money, too, to buy clothes, shoes, tools, and fertilizers, and to pay for medicine and school books. They sell some of their food crops, perhaps at the town market. They can also grow and sell **cash crops** such as coffee, tea, sugar, and cotton. More than half of the coffee and tea produced in Kenya is grown on small farms.

▽ Corn and beans growing on small farms in the highlands.

There are large farms in Kenya as well, for raising cattle and growing tea, coffee, and wheat. The company *Brooke Bond* owns huge plantations of tea bushes around Kericho. The green leaves are plucked and dried in nearby factories.

Most of the tea and coffee that Kenya grows is **exported**, which means it is sold and shipped to other countries. These two crops make up almost half of the money that Kenya earns from its exports. Kenya has to earn this money in order to pay for the things it buys from other countries. Some farmers are growing new export crops, such as French beans and chili peppers, strawberries and mangoes, and flowers.

On the drier lands that make up most of Kenya, people live differently. In the driest, or **arid**, areas, they keep **livestock** such as cows, sheep, goats, and camels. Families live off the milk, meat, and skins of their animals. These can also be sold at the market. Where there is a little more rainfall, farmers plant fast-growing cereal crops like millet and sorghum.

Women do much of the work in a farming family, both in the home and on the land. On small farms, the land is cultivated by hand with a tool called a hoe. Wealthier farmers may use a plow pulled by oxen or a tractor.

△ These women are picking coffee beans.

Industry

Kenya's industries are the most developed in East Africa. Some products are sold inside Kenya, and some are exported to neighboring countries like Uganda and Tanzania. In shops and markets, you can see names well known in the United States, such as *Colgate* toothpaste, *Lux* soap, *EverReady* batteries, and *Johnson's* baby powder. These are not **imports** from other countries; they are made in Kenya.

Most of Kenya's large industries were set up to process farm products. Corn is milled to produce flour, known as "unga." This is used in almost every home to cook ugali, a stiff porridge. Wheat flour is used to make bread and cakes in the town bakeries. Cotton is spun and woven to produce cloth. Other factories refine sugar from sugar cane, process milk and beef, use barley to brew beer, and process tobacco to make cigarettes.

Kenya has little coal, gas, or oil of its own. Much of the money that the country earns from its exports is spent on buying oil. Kenya also imports all of its iron and steel and most of the machinery used in its factories.

Many people make and sell things to earn a living. They become metalworkers, tailors, shoemakers, carpenters, flower sellers, or market traders. This is known as "Jua Kali," which means "hot sun," because they usually have to work outside in the hot sun!

Metal goods being made at Kamukunji Jua Kali.

The ceaseless clatter of hammers and chisels on metal echoes through Kamukunji Jua Kali in Nairobi. Behind stands crammed with shining goods, men are busy turning old oil drums and other scrap into lamps, cooking stoves, water heaters, buckets, bed frames, jugs, and cooking pots. There are few tools and no workbenches, just the dusty ground.

Tourists visit Amboseli Park to see the wildlife.

Tourism is another important source of **income** for Kenya and provides jobs for over 100,000 Kenyans. Every year half a million visitors come to spend their money at the beaches and wildlife parks. However, tourism has made life difficult for some Kenyans. To make space for the parks, herders like the Masai and Samburu have been thrown off the land where they used to live. But they receive very little of the money that the tourists spend.

Kenya's Challenge

Kenya does not have a large population for its size. But there is a shortage of good agricultural land. In a year of normal rainfall, Kenya can grow enough food for its people. In years of poor rainfall, like 1992–93, food has to be imported. Some of this food is sent by other countries as **food aid**.

△ Villagers giving out wheat and oil as food aid.

Poor Kenyans are the most likely to go without food, live in broken-down housing, and miss out on schooling and health care. Their **poverty** is not simply an accident. Like most African countries, Kenya is changing rapidly. These changes can make some groups of people more **vulnerable**, more likely to be pushed into poverty.

If families have land, they can produce their own food. In Kenya, land is not shared equally. White farmers took most of the best land when Kenya was ruled by Britain. When the country became independent, many of these farms were divided among small farmers. But almost half remain as large farms, owned by less than 4,000 wealthy Kenyan farmers.

The Masai and Samburu peoples live by herding livestock. But much of their best land is being taken for wildlife parks and for agriculture. This destroys their way of life, which depends on sharing vast areas of dry grazing land. The herders become less able to cope with drought, the periods of low rainfall that come every few years.

If you are a Kenyan woman, you are also much more likely to be poor. Women do more work than men but are less likely to have money, go to school, or take part in making decisions.

Disagreements that lead to fighting also bring poverty. Kenya has been a peaceful country. But since 1991, thousands of Kenyans have been driven from their homes by fighting in western Kenya. These clashes are linked to the shortage of agricultural land. But they have also been influenced by changes that introduced a **multi-party** political system in Kenya, similar to the one in the United States. Elections have caused tension between different groups in Kenya.

Kenyans will work to produce more food, to sell more goods to other countries, and to earn more from tourism. The challenge for the country is to achieve this without pushing more people to the edge of poverty. Above all, people everywhere in Kenya need to have a real say in the decisions that affect them and their way of life.

△ Women have the job of collecting water for the home.

Iltilal: A Masai Village

Iltilal is a village in southern Kenya, close to the border with Tanzania. It lies on a flat, grassy plain close to Tsavo National Park. Tsavo is the largest wildlife park in Kenya.

Most of the people in Iltilal are Masai. They are **pastoralists.** They make a living from their cows, goats, and sheep. There are many Masai villages like Iltilal in Kenya and Tanzania.

Most of the land around Iltilal is too dry to grow crops, but livestock can survive by moving from place to place in search of grass and shrubs. There are no fences. People make arrangements to share all the land.

In the dry season, between June and September, the land becomes bare and dusty. Only the thorny, wide-spreading acacia trees stay green, providing welcome shade in the middle of the day. At this time of year the cows have to be taken far from Iltilal to look for better grazing.

△ Iltilal during the rainy season.

The rains that come between October and May quickly make the land turn green. Livestock can feed close to the home, and milk is plentiful. Cattle can be sold and are killed and eaten on special occasions. But milk is the most important food in Iltilal.

There are about 200 homesteads in the village. A homestead is made up of several families who live together, each with their own house. They share the job of looking after the cows.

Inside each homestead, the houses are dotted in a rough circle around the main **boma**, or cattle enclosure. The boma is fenced with branches cut from thorn trees. At night this protects the cows against thieves and also predators such as lions.

Most houses are made from materials found in Iltilal. Walls and rafters are made from wooden poles tied together with string made from tree bark. The domed roof is covered with grass, and the walls are covered with mud and cow dung. There is no window. A single doorway winds into the house at an angle, like the entrance to a giant snail shell.

A dusty dirt road links Iltilal to the nearest town, Loitokitok, 37 miles away. In the other direction, the road leads into Tsavo Park. At the roadside in the village are a small shop and a tearoom, built with sheets of corrugated iron. Nearby is a Health Center, with a water pump used by the villagers. A little further from the main road are the primary school and the church.

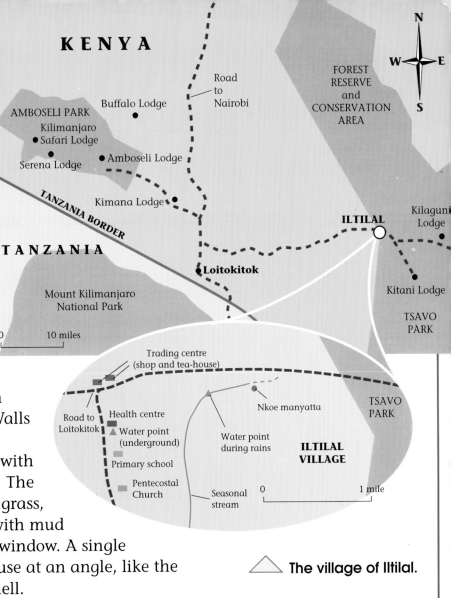

The village of Iltilal.

Taking cattle out of the homestead early in the morning.

Life in Iltilal

Women do most of the work around the homestead. It is a woman's job to build the house, milk the animals, and provide food and water for the family.

Children of about five years and older are expected to help. They care for younger children, collect water, wash dishes, and look after the calves. As they become older, girls work around the homestead with their mothers. Boys and young men take the cattle out to graze.

Older men make decisions that affect each homestead. They meet to discuss matters that affect the whole community of Iltilal. The local chief, Nkonina Songoi, was chosen as a leader when he was young. People respect his ideas.

▽ Families leaving Iltilal church after the Christmas service.

But things are changing in Iltilal. Elders must deal with government officials, who may have different ideas from them. The primary school has made a big difference in the lives of the children. At school they learn about Kenya and its history. They also learn English and Swahili, the national language.

The nurse at the Health Center has brought modern medical care to the village. Many of the girls at school now say they want to become nurses, too. The nearby town, Loitokitok, has grown rapidly. People in Iltilal can now sell and buy things more easily.

There are other changes that are more difficult for the villagers to cope with. In the dry season, the cattle used to be taken to better grazing land, where there was more rain. The land was kept especially for this purpose. Tsavo Park used to be the dry-season grazing land. But the Masai are no longer allowed to take cattle there in case they disturb the wild animals and the tourists. Other grazing areas have been taken by farmers to grow crops.

The Masai do not kill wild animals for meat. Zebra, giraffes, and antelope still roam across their land. They did not choose to have the game parks. Now there are new ideas about dividing and fencing the people's land. But who will make the decisions? Will it be business people in Loitokitok, or the government in Nairobi? Or will the people of Iltilal be allowed to make their own choices?

△ Women like Nonkipa do most of the work around the homestead. Here she is with her baby and her niece Tido.

Education

The number of schools has grown rapidly since Kenya became an independent country in 1963. Children start school when they are about six years old. Most spend eight years at primary school, passing from Standard One to Standard Eight.

Some children drop out of school because their parents need their help at home. This happens most in country areas like Iltilal, where schools have only been built in recent years. In the past, children had their schooling at home, learning the skills needed to look after cattle or grow crops.

Now things are changing. Nice Nkoe is fifteen years old. She is the first girl to reach Standard Eight at Iltilal School, but many more will follow. Her cousin Consolata, who is twelve, in Standard Five, is likely to be one. "I'd hate anyone who tried to stop me from going to school," she said. "I miss it during the holidays."

▷ New classrooms being built at Iltilal School.

△ Nice and Kilesi setting off for school.

Nice usually walks to school with her cousins and her sister, Mankushai, who is ten. They leave home at about 7:30 A.M. to reach school in time for the start of class at 8:00 A.M. They have a one-hour lunch break and finish at 3:45 P.M. All the children wear school uniforms.

Nice and her cousin, Kilesi, are just finishing Standard Eight. They have taken the important final exams that all children complete in the last year of primary school.

Nice enjoys school. "My favorite subject is English. Today we read *A Visit to Turkana*. It's interesting because none of us has ever been there. The Turkana people keep cows, but they're very different from the Masai!"

"We spend most time on science and GHC (Geography, History, and Civics). We learn a lot about Kenya. Then there's math, Swahili, and religious education. We don't do many sports—the teachers say it's too hot. They aren't from Masailand!"

Nice has plans for her future. "I want to be a doctor or a nurse, so I can work in Loitokitok hospital and help the people who live in this area. First I have to get to secondary school. I'll need high scores in my exams to get there."

Children spend four years in secondary school. There is only room for one of every five children, and parents have to pay part of the cost.

△ Nice and Hamisi share a book during their English lesson.

Spare Time

In Iltilal, the younger children play games that are found almost everywhere in the world. They might start playing tag as they look after the calves, or draw lines in the dirt to see who can jump the furthest.

Consolata describes other popular games: "We make houses. We can use sticks and grass, or just stones to mark the walls. Someone acts as mother, someone as father, others as the children. We play ball games like kati. We stand in a circle and try to hit the person in the middle."

Days are spent outside, because the climate is warm. The children have lots of space and lots of freedom. They do not have to be warned about talking to strangers or being careful about how they cross the road. They just have to watch out for snakes, and possibly even lions!

△ Consolata leads a dancing game. She is facing you.

◁ A women's group singing at the harambee.

▷ Bao is a popular game in Kenya.

Nice and Consolata both sing in the school choir. In her last month at primary school, Nice led the choir at a harambee. This was a local show to raise money for the school. About $1,600 was collected! "Harambee" means people joining together to help themselves.

At school, children like to play soccer, netball (a kind of basketball), and volleyball. Kenyans are great runners, too. In the 1992 Olympics, Kenya won gold medals in the men's 800, 1500, 3000, and 5000 meter races.

As they grow up, most Kenyan children have a different idea of play than children in Europe or the United States. Work and play are not separate. "We enjoy ourselves when we go out together to collect wood or water," Nice explained. "It's not hard work."

An important reason for this big difference is that Kenyan children are usually part of a close-knit family. They think more of doing things for their families than doing things for themselves. Jobs are usually shared with

brothers, sisters, cousins, or friends, giving the children a chance to chat and joke together. There are always aunts, uncles, and grandparents to turn to for advice.

In the large towns life is different. For those who have money, there are movie theaters and restaurants, swimming pools and sports centers, fairgrounds, and video games. But family relationships can become less important to people when they move to a town.

A Day with the Nkoe Family

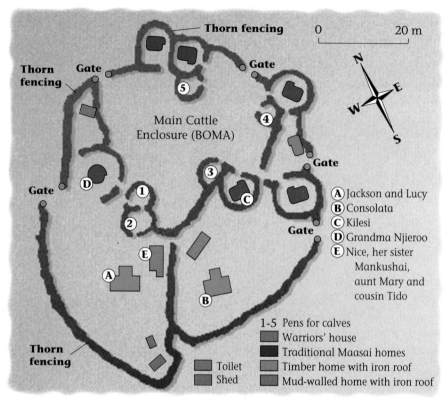

Thorn fencing

0   20 m

Thorn fencing   Gate   Gate

Main Cattle Enclosure (BOMA)

Gate

Gate

Gate   Gate

(A) Jackson and Lucy
(B) Consolata
(C) Kilesi
(D) Grandma Njieroo
(E) Nice, her sister Mankushai, aunt Mary and cousin Tido

Thorn fencing

1-5 Pens for calves
     Warriors' house
     Traditional Maasai homes
     Timber home with iron roof
     Mud-walled home with iron roof

Toilet
Shed

◁ Where people live in the Nkoe manyatta, Iltilal.

▷ Lucy and Mary cooking ugali and potatoes in the kitchen.

▽ Lucy and Jackson outside their timber bungalow.

Work in the homestead begins before sunrise. The women are up first, moving quietly through the gray half-light. A smell of smoke hangs in the still air as fires are lit in the kitchens. Cows begin to stir in the boma.

Nice gets washed and dressed. Usually she would be getting ready for school. But it is late November, and the schools have closed for the long holiday.

Nice greets her mother, Lucy, and aunt Mary. She then goes out to collect water with her younger sister, Mankushai, and her cousins, Tido and Consolata. After recent good rainfall, they can fill their containers from the small stream close to the homestead.

Nice's cousin, Kilesi, is also up early. He helps to open the cattle gates and take the cows out of the homestead. Nice comes back to join the women, who are milking the cows in the early morning sunshine. There are over 200 cows, but each woman knows which are hers.

In the kitchen Nice's grandmother, Njieroo, and Tido drink mugs of milk still warm from the cows. Milk and sugar are boiled to make tea. Nice takes a mug to her father, Jackson. For those who want it, there's ugali from the previous evening. Ugali is boiled cornmeal, broken off and eaten with the fingers, like bread.

Kilesi and his brothers take the cattle towards the Chyulu Hills to find the best grazing. The younger boys and girls take the calves to graze close to the homestead.

The homestead is quiet in the heat of the day. Jackson talks with his brothers and other elders. He is employed by the government to watch out for poachers around Tsavo Park.

Nice washes clothes, helped by Tido. As the day cools, Nice and her aunt Mary go to collect more water. The calves are brought back to their pens, and as the sun sets, the young herders return with the cattle. Nice comes to milk her family's cows again, this time inside the homestead. The light fades quickly. As the mosquitoes start to bite, people move indoors and sit around the fire.

Jackson lights an oil lamp. The men are fed first and eat separately. The women and children eat in the kitchen by the light of the cooking fire. The day ends as it started—with the sounds of the women working, cleaning the plates and pots.

Travel Around Iltilal

Nice and Lucy at the market in Loitokitok.

Pastoralists like the Masai are very good walkers. They think nothing of walking almost 25 miles in a day to tend cattle or visit relatives.

In Iltilal, most of the things people need are within walking distance. People walk to the water pump, to the shop, to the woods, to school, to the Health Center, and to church. Donkeys are used as "burden" animals, to carry water, firewood, and other goods. They are essential when families move their homes.

Nice collects water in Iltilal and walks home. The concrete tank is filled with water pumped from underground.

People in Iltilal do not own cars. But the world of rapid travel, of airplanes and cars, does reach into Iltilal. Every week, dozens of mini-vans hurry through the village, bringing tourists from Europe and America to Tsavo Park. They rarely stop to talk to the villagers. "They come and they leave knowing nothing about us," says Chief Songoi.

Loitokitok is the nearest town to Iltilal. People go there to buy the things they cannot easily get in the village, such as cornmeal and tea, sugar and salt, clothes and shoes, cooking pots, bowls, and mugs. Nice and her mother travel to town about once a month, when they can get a lift with a truck or van.

At first the rough dirt road to Loitokitok passes through grassland similar to Iltilal. There are few vehicles apart from tourist vans. As the road climbs gently towards Loitokitok, the landscape changes. Groups of women are sowing corn and beans in plowed fields. There is better rainfall here. This used to be pastoralist land, kept for grazing cows in the dry season. Now farmers have bought it and fenced it off.

Tourist mini-vans traveling in convoy towards Tsavo Park from Loitokitok.

Loitokitok lies on the lower slope of Kilimanjaro, Africa's highest mountain. After heavy overnight rain, young men push wooden wheelbarrows through the mud. They are paid to carry goods to the market. Small minibuses arrive at the market entrance, their roofs piled high with boxes and bags of vegetables and fruit. In the market, produce is set out on sacks. There might be beans, carrots, peas, cabbages, tomatoes, potatoes, oranges, mangos, and bananas. Most of the buyers and sellers are women.

Nice buys a dress from one of the shops. Lucy buys some vegetables and cornmeal. By the time they leave, the town has fallen under the shadow of Kilimanjaro.

Travel Around Kenya

Most travel in Kenya is on foot, especially in country areas. Turkana women like Arukudi Lobe will travel more than 60 miles to collect wild fruits. "We walk for two or three days, beyond these hills as far as Kokuro, before returning on the fourth day. We carry home soft fruits like emeyen, ekalale, edome, elero, and eng'omo. And edung and edapal, which have to be boiled with fire ash."

Pastoralists often pack up their homesteads and move with their livestock. Then they use donkeys or camels to carry the young children and the mats and poles from which they build their homes.

Bikes are used widely too, although it is often frowned on for women to ride them except as passengers sitting sideways on the crossbar. Around Lake Victoria, men ride home with huge fish called Nile perch draped across their bikes. Sometimes a bike may be so heavily loaded that it has to be pushed, not ridden. It might be carrying 45 pounds of cotton or bananas.

△ **Kenyatta Avenue in Nairobi. The word "uhuru" on the banner means "freedom."**

Machakos Bus Station in Nairobi.

Most people use buses to get around town. The brightly painted buses are called matatus or manyangas. Kenyans crowding onto the packed buses to get to and from work will sometimes wait for their favorite manyanga, perhaps one with a careful driver or the softest seats and best music system.

Buses are the most popular way of moving around the country. Those who want to travel out of Nairobi go to "Machakos Airport," the name jokingly given to the city's busy Machakos Bus Station. This is the noisy, colorful starting point for long journeys into the country, as Kenyans working in the city go back home to see relatives and friends.

Less than one out of every hundred people in Kenya owns a car, but cities like Nairobi, Mombasa, and Nakuru still have traffic jams.

Kenya's main railroad line links the port of Mombasa to Kisumu and Kampala, the capital of Uganda. The railroad was built by the British between 1896 and 1904 to open up trade. It seems incredible that Kenya's modern capital, Nairobi, began its life then as a railroad camp.

Images of Kenya

Everywhere you travel in Kenya, you can find Kenyans working to meet the challenges that face the country.

If you visited Machakos, you might hear Kyungu women's group singing while they work together to improve their fields. They have built terraces, which are earth banks that stretch across the hillsides. The terraces trap the rain and stop it from washing the soil downhill. "When we plant corn, beans, and onions, they are bigger in size now," explains Munjira Maleve. There are thousands of groups like Kyungu, and they have terraced most of the land in Machakos.

△ A meeting of people with disabilities in Wajir. Asia Mude is closest to the camera.

In Wajir town, you would be welcomed and asked to sit in the sunshine and talk to people with disabilities who have formed an Association. "On my own, I couldn't do anything," explains Asia Mude. "But when lots of us get together, we can urge the government to provide proper services." Geddo Ali, who like Asia is blind, is about to begin teaching at Wajir Secondary School. "I'm going to encourage parents to send children with disabilities to the school. I want to show them that they can manage on their own—like me!"

In Busia in western Kenya, you might meet Margaret Afandi riding her bike to call on her neighbors. Margaret and her husband grow all their family's food on just 1.2 acres of land. They also have more than 100 chickens' eggs to sell each day. Margaret is an **organic** farmer. She uses manure and compost on her land rather than expensive fertilizers. Now she spends time visiting neighbors to pass on her ideas.

▷ A women's group collecting stones to build a shop.

And back again in Wajir, ten-year-old Ibrahim Sheikh might come over to talk to you. His family lost all their camels and goats and have come to live close to the town. They cannot afford to pay anything towards Ibrahim's schooling. "But I'm top of the class!" Ibrahim says proudly.

Thinking perhaps that you might not believe him, Ibrahim runs to his home about 2 miles away. Less than an hour later, he comes panting back with a sheet of paper which he carefully unfolds. "See, 'Position in class: 1,'" he laughs.

If Kenya can provide schooling for all its children, it will be better able to meet the challenges of the future.

Glossary

Arid Dry, having little rain. In Kenya areas which receive less than 8 inches of rain each year are officially described as arid.

Cash crops Crops that are grown to be sold rather than eaten by the farmers themselves. This can include food crops, such as vegetables or corn, which can be taken to a nearby town market or sold to traders. Coffee and tea are important cash crops that are grown mainly for selling to other countries.

Culture A people's whole way of life. This includes their ideas, beliefs, language, values, knowledge, customs, and the things they make.

Exports Goods sold and transported to other countries.

Food aid Food given to those who are unable to provide for themselves. Food aid is usually given by one country to another, either directly or through the United Nations World Food Program. Corn and wheat are most commonly used for food aid.

Herder Someone who looks after a herd of animals, such as cows, camels, sheep, or goats.

Hydroelectric station A place where machinery produces electricity from flowing water. In Kenya, rivers are dammed to produce a strong flow of water. In some countries, the ebb and flow of sea tides is used to make electricity.

Imports Goods brought in from other countries.

Income Money received. Tourism, and the sale of exports such as tea and coffee, bring money into Kenya. This provides income for Kenyan workers and for the government.

Independent Not depending on others, free to act or make decisions. A country is said to be independent when it is free to govern itself and is not ruled by another country.

Livestock Animals such as cows, goats, camels, sheep, and pigs kept by farmers or herders.

Matatu Small private bus or minivan. The word comes from "tatu," which in Swahili means "three," because the original fare in Nairobi was three cents. Bigger, brightly painted buses with soft seats and loud music systems are call "manyangas."

Missionaries People who are sent by their church to do religious work in a foreign country. Early missionaries brought Christianity to Africans.

Multi-party A political system that allows more than one political party. Until 1991 Kenya was a one-party state, ruled by the Kenya African National Union (KANU). The first multi-party election was held in 1992.

Organic farmer A farmer who grows crops using fertilizers and pest-killers made from or by plants and animals. For example, animal manure and compost made from rotted plants are used as fertilizers. In this way, the farmer avoids the dangers of artificial chemical products and also saves money.

Pastoralists People who mainly depend on livestock to make their living. They use the milk, meat, and blood of their animals for food. Other animal products, such as skins, are sold or used to make clothes, houses, tools, and containers. Pastoralists are often nomadic, traveling long distances to find fresh grazing for their animals.

Poverty The condition of being poor. People can be reduced to poverty if their way of life is threatened or if they do not have enough land, money, or other resources to enjoy a reasonable standard of life. Poverty differs from one country to another. People in the United States may feel they are poor if they do not own a car or a TV. Only wealthy people in Kenya would hope to own such things.

Temperate Moderate, not extreme. A temperate climate is one which is neither very hot nor very cold.

Vulnerable Unprotected, easily hurt or damaged. For example, if farmers cannot save enough money or harvest good crops, they become vulnerable. Poor rainfall and one bad harvest may push them into poverty.

Index

About Oxfam in Kenya

Oxfam America works in partnership with communities in Asia, Africa, the Americas, and the Caribbean to find long term solutions to poverty and hunger. Oxfam America supports the self-help efforts of poor people—especially women, landless farm workers, and survivors of war and natural disasters—who are working to make their lives better. Oxfam America believes that all people have the basic rights to earn a living and to have food, shelter, health care, and education.

Oxfam America is part of the international family of Oxfam organizations that work in more than 70 countries, including Kenya, where Oxfam's program encourages poor people to consider the causes of their poverty and to take action to improve their circumstances. This requires investment in people, to inspire confidence and impart practical and organizational skills. Oxfam uses this approach in its four main areas of work in Kenya. Oxfam works with women to ensure that they are involved in all projects and with pastoralists—nomadic people—to promote community-based health care. Oxfam also works with farmers in areas with poor soil and inconsistent rainfall to help them produce enough food for their families.

© 1996 Rigby Education
Published by Rigby Interactive Library,
an imprint of Rigby Education,
division of Reed Elsevier, Inc.
500 Coventry Lane
Crystal Lake, IL 60014

Printed in Hong Kong
Designed and produced by Visual Image
Cover design by Threefold Design

00 99 98 97 96
10 9 8 7 6 5 4 3 2 1

Library of Congress Cataloging-in-Publication Data

Marshall, David, 1945 Apr. 12--
    Kenya / David Marshall, Geoff Sayer.
        p.   cm. -- (Worldfocus)
    Includes index.
    ISBN 1-57572-027-2
    1. Kenya--Juvenile literature. I. Sayer, Geoff.
II.Title. III. Series.
DT433.522.M39 1996
967.62--dc20   95-25032

Acknowledgments

The author and publishers would like to thank the following for their help with this book: Oxfam (UK and Ireland) Geoff Sayer who took on the role of co-author at very short notice; Ian Leggett and the staff of the East Africa Desk; the staff of the photo library; and the Oxfam Education workers who commented on early drafts; the people of Iltilal; and the staff at the Oxfam Nairobi office.

The author and publishers also wish to acknowledge, with thanks, the following photographic sources:

Goeff Sayer/Oxfam pp. 2, 3, 5, 8, 10–29; Peter Barker/Panos Pictures p. 4; J. Spafford/Oxfam p. 9; Karen Twining/Oxfam p. 29.

Every effort has been made to contact copyright holders of material published in this book. Any omissions will be rectified in subsequent printings if notice is given to the publisher.

Cover photograph: © Oxfam/Geoff Sayer—Turkana children in northern Kenya